SUPER SHARKS

GREAT WHITE

Dan Lopez

NorwoodHouse Press

Cataloging-in-Publication Data

Names: Lopez, Dan.
Title: Great white / Dan Lopez.
Description: Buffalo, NY : Norwood House Press, 2027. | Series: Super sharks | Includes glossary and index.
Identifiers: ISBN 9781978581319 (pbk.) | ISBN 9781978581326 (library bound) | ISBN 9781978581333 (ebook)
Subjects: LCSH: White shark--Juvenile literature.
Classification: LCC QL638.95.L3 L67 2027 | DDC 597.33--dc23

Published in 2027 by
Norwood House Press
2544 Clinton Street
Buffalo, NY 14224

Designer: Rhea Magaro
Editor: Tricia Hoffman

Photo credits: Cover, pp. 1, 11 Alessandro De Maddalena/Shutterstock.com; p. 4 Everett Collection/Shutterstock.com; pp. 5, 17-19 Sergey Uryadnikov/Shutterstock.com; p. 6 Wirestock Creators/Shutterstock.com; p. 9 ckabir/Shutterstock.com; p. 10 anaspng/Shutterstock.com; p. 12 Petra Christen/Shutterstock.com; p. 15 Jennifer Mellon Photos/Shutterstock.com; p. 21 Tanya_Terekhina/Shutterstock.com;

Printed in the United States of America

TABLE OF CONTENTS

What Is Special about Great Whites?

The great white may be the most well-known shark on Earth. It starred in the famous movie *Jaws*.

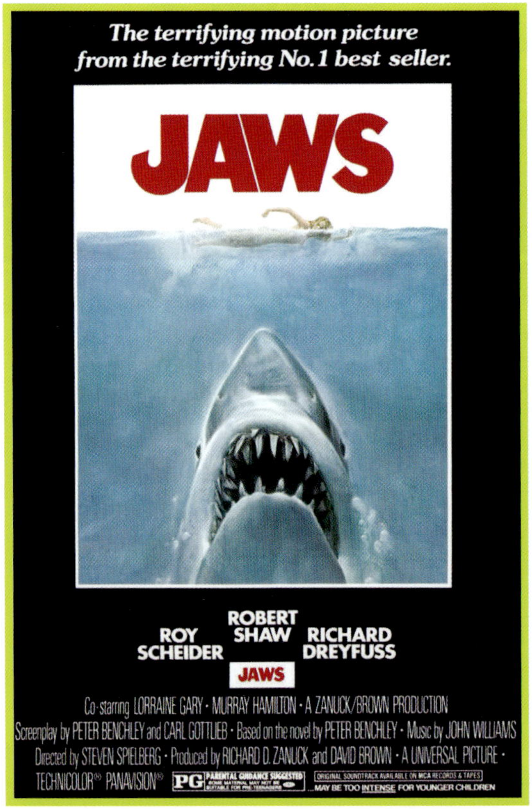

Great whites are **apex predators**. These giant fish have giant teeth that are ready to attack. They don't hunt humans. A great white will rarely bite a person.

WHAT DO GREAT WHITES LOOK LIKE?

Great whites are the world's largest predatory fish. They can be more than 20 feet (six meters) long. They can weigh 4,500 pounds (2,040 kilograms).

A great white gets its name from its white belly. The top of its body is brownish-gray. Its colors provide **camouflage**. Seen from above, the shark blends in with the water. Seen from below, it blends in with the sunlight.

The great white has a big mouth! It contains up to seven rows of teeth with about 300 teeth in all. Each triangle-shaped, **serrated** tooth has a sharp point.

There are two **dorsal fins**. The front one is larger. Sometimes, it sticks out above the water.

Where Do Great Whites Live?

Great whites live in oceans around the world. They like **tropical** and **temperate** waters.

Young great whites stay closer to coasts. Adults swim in the open sea.

How Do Great Whites Hunt?

Great whites are great hunters. They see and hear well. They smell **prey** from miles away. They sense **vibrations** made by other animals. They can swim more than 31 miles (50 kilometers) per hour over short distances.

Young great whites eat fish and rays. Adults hunt **mammals** such as sea lions and seals.

Great whites make surprise attacks from below. They may **breach** the water to catch a meal.

Great whites don't chew. They rip off chunks of meat and swallow them whole.

How Do Great Whites Reproduce?

Females give birth to live babies, or pups. Up to 17 are born at once. As soon as they are born, pups swim away. They don't want their mother to eat them!

GLOSSARY

apex predators (AY-peks PRED-uh-turz): animals at the top of the food chain that hunt other animals but are not hunted by other animals

breach (breech): to suddenly jump out of the water

camouflage (KAM-uh-flahzh): a disguise or natural coloring that lets animals hide by making them look like their surroundings

dorsal fins (DOR-sl fins): flat, thin body parts that stick up from the back of a shark or other marine animal

mammals (MAM-uhlz): animals that have backbones and fur or hair, that give birth to live babies, and that feed their babies milk from the mother

prey (pray): animals eaten by other animals

serrated (SER-ay-ted): notched like the blade of a saw

temperate (TEM-pur-it): having temperatures that are rarely very high or very low

tropical (TRAH-pi-kuhl): near or having to do with the hot and rainy area near Earth's equator

vibrations (vye-BRAY-shuhnz): rapid movements

Thinking Questions

1. Why are great whites so well-known?
2. How did the great white get its name?
3. Describe a great white's teeth.
4. What makes the great white such a good hunter?
5. What do great whites eat?

INDEX

ABOUT THE AUTHOR

Dan Lopez lives far from the ocean in Indianapolis, Indiana, with his wife and three kids. He is fascinated by all of Earth's animals, including sharks! He admires their sleekness and speed and thinks more people should appreciate them.